Reminiscences of

General James H. Doolittle

U.S. Air Force (Retired)

U.S. Naval Institute

Annapolis, Maryland

1987

PREFACE

The story of James H. Doolittle and the air raid he led on Japan in April 1942 is well known by students of World War II. In this brief memoir, General Doolittle fills in many details about this daring, morale-building mission.

As a lieutenant colonel, Doolittle first learned about a budding plan to launch an air attack on Tokyo from his boss, Lieutenant General Hap Arnold, Chief of the Army Air Forces, in January 1942. Through his ingenuity, he was able to convince Arnold to let him lead the raid, despite the general's feelings that Doolittle was too valuable an asset to his staff to be released. Doolittle covers this mission from the earliest planning stages through June 1942, when he was presented the Medal of Honor by President Franklin Roosevelt. He also discusses the preparations and training necessary to allow Army pilots to fly from a carrier, the mechanics of the B-25 bombers flown during the raid, and service relationships, both during the mission and throughout his career.

Thanks go to Captain Paul B. Ryan, USN (Ret.), who conducted this interview at General Doolittle's office in Monterey, California, and to Deborah Reid of the Naval Institute staff who did the transcribing and smooth typing.

Susan B. Sweeney
Oral History Department
U.S. Naval Institute
September 1987

Authorization

The U.S. Naval Institute is hereby authorized to make available to individuals, libraries and other repositories of its choosing the transcript of the oral history interview concerning the life and career of the undersigned. The interview was recorded on 15 February 1983, in collaboration with Captain Paul B. Ryan, U.S. Navy (Retired), for the U.S. Naval Institute.

The undersigned does hereby release and assign to the U.S. Naval Institute all right, title, restriction, and interest in the interview. The copyright in both the oral and transcribed versions shall be the sole property of the U.S. Naval Institute. The tape recording of the interview is and will remain the property of the U.S. Naval Institute.

Signed and sealed this ___third___ day of ___August___ 1987.

James H. Doolittle
General, U.S. Air Force (Retired)

Interview with General James H. Doolittle,
         U.S. Air Force (Retired)

Place: General Doolittle's office, Monterey, California

Date: 15 February 1983

Subject: Biography

Interviewer: Captain Paul B. Ryan, U.S. Navy (Retired)

Q: General Doolittle, going back to January 1942, the idea of the raid was first raised by General Arnold with you, and you had no prior knowledge of it. Is that so?*

General Doolittle: That is correct. The raid, as I understand it, was conceived--the idea was conceived by Captain (later Vice Admiral) Low.** He took it to Admiral King.*** Admiral King and General Marshall discussed it with General Arnold.**** They were all enthusiastic about it. They then went to the President with the idea, and he approved enthusiastically.***** I was on

---

    *Lieutenant General Henry H. Arnold, USA, Chief of the U.S. Army Air Forces; Arnold, who headed the Army Air Forces throughout World War II, was promoted to general in March 1943 and general of the Army in December 1944.
    **Captain Francis S. Low, USN.
    ***Admiral Ernest J. King, USN, Commander in Chief U.S. Fleet from December 1941 to October 1945 and Chief of Naval Operations from March 1942 to December 1945. King was promoted to fleet admiral in December 1944.
    ****General George C. Marshall, USA, Army Chief of Staff from 1939 to 1945. Marshall was promoted to general of the Army in December 1944.
    *****Franklin D. Roosevelt, President of the United States from 1933 to 1945.

General Arnold's staff, and he called me in to make the necessary arrangements to select and modify the aircraft, to select and train the crews.

Q: Then the President knew of the general plan, but he didn't know the exact date, did he? Because I understand Admiral King told him after you were launched of the details of this raid. Does that sound correct?

General Doolittle: I do not know how much the President knew. There was, as you remember, a little difficulty in getting Chiang Kai-shek's approval for us to land in China, because he knew that the Japanese would take a very dim view of that.* So my understanding is that Chiang Kai-shek was not notified until the task force was under way, lest he make a strong effort to call it off.

Q: The actual planning for the raid was done by Captain Donald Duncan, known as Wu Duncan. Is that correct?**

General Doolittle: It is my understanding that the concept was

---

*Chiang Kai-shek, Generalissimo (1887-1975), supreme commander of Allied air and land forces in China from January 1942 to October 1943, when he became President of the Nationalist Government.
**Captain Donald B. Duncan, USN, whose oral history is in the Columbia University collection. Duncan, eventually a four-star admiral, was Vice Chief of Naval Operations from 1951 to 1956.

then-Captain (later Vice Admiral) Low's, that he and then-Captain (later Admiral) Duncan made the preliminary plans.

Q: You had assistance, of course, in planning the target choices. Do you recall how that was done?

General Doolittle: Yes. Aboard the Hornet was Captain Jurika, who had been a naval air attache in Tokyo.* He was very well versed in the most desirable targets, and he briefed us carefully on targeting. Targets were selected according to the targets that would do the most damage to Japan and also carefully avoiding the Imperial Palace and anything that could cause unfair criticism.

Q: Well, Captain Davey Jones in your command was helpful, I understand, in getting target folders and charts and maps together.** Do you recall that he was of assistance?

General Doolittle: I don't remember the details of it.

Q: But after General Arnold briefed you, then it was a closed door, for your command knew nothing of this.

---
*Captain Stephen Jurika, Jr., USN (Ret.), whose oral history is part of the Naval Institute collection. He was a lieutenant in 1942.
**Captain David M. Jones, USA, one of the pilots who flew in the raid. Jones's recollections are contained in Lieutenant Colonel Carroll V. Glines, USAF, Doolittle's Tokyo Raiders (Princeton, New Jersey: D. Van Nostrand Company, Inc., 1964).

General Doolittle: I was on his staff, and he gave me the job, as I said, of making the necessary preparations and supervising the training. When we were about halfway through with the training, I requested permission to lead the flight, and he at first refused and then later agreed that I might lead it.

Q: Well, who else do you think he had in mind, General, if he didn't have you to go?

General Doolittle: When I asked to lead it, he said he wanted me on his staff, and he didn't say who he was going to have lead it.

Q: Well, I have to say it's fortunate that you led it. I don't know anybody else who could do it.

General Doolittle: My story to him was that I knew more about the raid than anyone else, knew more about the people, knew more about the aircraft. Consequently, I would like very much to lead it.

Q: One of your stipulations to your command was, "You will not hit the Imperial Palace."

General Doolittle: I directly ordered each individual personally to avoid hitting the Imperial Palace. The principal reason for that was that the Germans had either advertently or inadvertently bombed Buckingham Palace, and this steeled the British people as nothing else could. If it was a mistake, it was a costly mistake to the Germans, because it had a profound effect in pulling the British solidly together.

Q: In other words, it would have been a psychological penalty for us.

General Doolittle: It would have been a psychological penalty as well as the wrong thing to do.

Q: In your planning for the raid, did you anticipate that the Japanese had radar?

General Doolittle: We did not think they had radar. There was, however, the possibility that they might have, and our intelligence was not sufficiently good to tell us whether they had none, some rudimentary capabilities, or a considerable capability. We presumed that they might.

Q: I'm getting ahead of the story, but I'll ask it now since we're on the subject. When you launched from the Hornet and you led the aircraft in, did you home in on the Tokyo radio with

RDF?*

General Doolittle: No, we did strictly dead reckoning, and we did not go in in formation. We went in one at a time in line as we took off from the carrier. Some of the chaps did overtake each other and end up with maybe a couple or three airplanes together. The reason we did not fly in formation was twofold. First, then the ones that were all first would have to wait for about an hour, and they'd use up an hour of gasoline waiting for the last one off. More important than that, you can fly individually using much less gas than you fly in formation because in formation, you're continually--unless you're the leader--continually jockeying. One airplane did form on me after we left Japan, flew all the way to the coast with me.

Q: At the time in early January when this raid plan was developing, I understand there was a lot of public opinion pressure on the Navy Department after things got bad in the Philippines, and the Western world lost Hong Kong, Singapore, and so forth. The cry was, "Where is the U.S. Navy? Why don't they do something?" And this raid was spurred by this pressure. Do you recall this thinking?

---

*RDF--radio direction finder

General Doolittle: We had been on the defensive, and the nation badly needed an offensive action. And so it was timely from that point of view.

Q: Did you meet Admiral King while the planning was going on?

General Doolittle: I met Admiral King from time to time. I don't know whether I specifically met him and reported to him on the planning or not.

Q: Did you see Captain Duncan occasionally?

General Doolittle: From time to time.

Q: Your office was in the Munitions Building right next door to Main Navy, was it not?*

General Doolittle: My office was in the Munitions Building, but I did not utilize that office but very little during the time that we were preparing the aircraft.

Q: You were all over the country, I suppose.

---

*These two buildings, the headquarters of the Army and Navy respectively, were on Constitution Avenue in Washington, D.C.

General Doolittle: I was a bird of passage.

Q: Yes, I knew the modifications to the B-25s were going on in the Midwest somewhere, were they not?

General Doolittle: Well, up around Detroit and through that area where there were a lot of . . .

Q: You were commuting from Eglin Field to Washington a lot, I suppose.*

General Doolittle: That's right.

Q: Did you meet Captain Low at all during the planning?

General Doolittle: I must have met him, but I don't remember any specific time, though.

Q: Can you give a thumbnail sketch of Admiral King, Captain Duncan, and Captain Low--just characteristics that might have struck you?

General Doolittle: Well, they're all very competent and very definite individuals.

---
*Eglin Field, now Eglin Air Force Base, in Valparaiso, Florida.

Q: You didn't sense the aloof chilliness that Admiral King projected, did you?

General Doolittle: Well, I was a "light colonel," and my associations with Admiral King were minimal. Any association with him would be through General Arnold, my boss.

Q: Another random question here. Spencer Tracy and Van Johnson made a movie, Thirty Seconds Over Tokyo.* Did you agree it was a true projection or depiction of the operation?

General Doolittle: I saw the premiere in London. I was in England when the picture was finished. There were several of the boys acted as consultants during the making of the picture, and I thought, frankly, that it was an excellent picture.

Q: Good. The naval officer who was assigned to train your group in carrier takeoffs was Lieutenant Henry "Hank" Miller, who was of class of '34 at the Naval Academy.** You recall your first meeting with Lieutenant Miller, General?

---

*Thirty Seconds Over Tokyo was released by the Metro-Goldwyn-Mayer in January 1945. It was based on a book of the same title by Ted W. Lawson (New York: Random House, Inc., 1943).
**Lieutenant Miller retired as a rear admiral in August 1971. His oral history, in the Naval Institute collection, contains his action report from the Doolittle Raid as an appendix.

General Doolittle: Yes, very well indeed. We discussed one thing and another, and somehow it came out that we were both old sourdoughs from Alaska--he from Fairbanks and I from Nome. I believe he was born in Alaska. I went up there at the ripe old age of three, and this was a very close bond between us.

Q: Did you discuss his background in athletics?

General Doolittle: Yes, as we discussed our respective backgrounds, I found that we had both been boxers. So we had a great deal in common. To this day we're very good friends. He honors us by coming to the reunions each year. This year, by the way, the reunion will be here in this area.

Q: In Carmel?

General Doolittle: Yes, and I'm looking forward with pleasant anticipation to some time with Hank.

Q: With regards to the sport of boxing, did you consider it valuable training for flight training?

General Doolittle: I feel that two things were very helpful to me in my flying career. One was tumbling, where you get a sense of balance. And the other was boxing, where unless you get pretty badly mauled, your reactions have to be extremely quick. So the balance and the quick reactions that come from boxing and tumbling, I think, were definitely helpful to me in my career.

Q: Going on to the choice of the 17th Bombardment Group for your mission to Tokyo, General Arnold, I suppose, made that decision, did he not?

General Doolittle: When I was given this job by General Arnold, he gave me the most valuable thing that anybody running a project can have in the military--that's top priority. I had top priority, and he gave me complete control. When he turned the job over to me, he didn't interfere in any way. So the first thing I did was to find out which group had had the most experience in flying B-25s. The 17th Group had had more experience than any other. And so I went to the 17th Group and asked for volunteers for a dangerous mission, not telling them what it was. And the entire group, including the group commander, volunteered. So I got an operations officer and a deputy commander and turned over to them the selection of crews, and they better than anyone else knew the capabilities of each group. And so we picked over crews and selected 24. We were only going to use 16, so we had a 50% buffer to make sure that if anything happened to some of the crews, why, we would still have plenty. As a matter of fact, two of the crews cracked up in training--nobody hurt. They washed out their airplanes. That was on the short takeoffs.

Q: You had 22 aircraft then as backup, with the 16 you used. Is that correct?

General Doolittle: That's correct.

Q: And you showed up, I think, in Alameda with 22 B-25s and took 16?

General Doolittle: That's right. And we took the crews from all of the aircraft on the carrier so that we would have those spare crews aboard. So there were, I guess, 22. I don't think we took the two crews that had washed out aboard the carrier. I'm not sure, but I know we took the other 22. We would only use 16.

Q: So you had 70 officers and 130 enlisted men, according to the records on board the Hornet. Well, this says a lot for the training and morale of this group, and it was, I think, valuable. You may have considered this. I'll ask you if you did. If you had taken pilots from various squadrons, there wouldn't have been a sense of unity of command and morale. Did this come into your thinking?

General Doolittle: It was certainly a distinct advantage to be able to get them all from more or less the same place because they all knew each other and they had all sort of sized each other up. They didn't have to do that after we started the specified training.

Q: When you flew from Eglin Field after training for carrier takeoffs, you flew to Sacramento for final tune-ups. You also, I understand, did some more polishing up on carrier takeoffs at Willows, California, which is 20 miles from Chico. Can you tell me about Willows? Did you have an Army airfield there, or how did you choose it?

General Doolittle: Willows had a rather small airfield there, and one of my lifelong friends was a crop duster at Willows. We dropped in more or less to see him when we went to Willows. There was no other reason.

Q: That was a happy circumstance then. This story is new, and I've never seen this come out before.

When you went aboard the Hornet at Alameda, you were greeted by Captain Mitscher and Commander Apollo Soucek, Commander George Henderson, and Commander Frank Akers, all ship's officers and old aviation early birds, I guess is the word.* You knew them all before, did you not?

General Doolittle: I did not know any of them well. I had in the Schneider Trophy Races in 1925--I met some of the Navy folks who flew in the races.** I don't believe that I had met Captain Mitscher before. If I had, it has now slipped my memory. But I knew some of the other people either personally or by reputation.

Q: Well, they knew who you were, I'm sure, and you were warmly greeted on board. Captain Mitscher turned over his cabin, and then he took his sea cabin. Is that correct?

General Doolittle: When we went aboard, there was perhaps just the least bit of coolness between the Navy people and the Army people. We felt a little out of place on a carrier, and they felt a little out of place having us there. But when we went under the San Francisco Bridge, over the radio said, "Hear ye,

---

*Captain Marc A. Mitscher, USN, Naval Aviator #33, commanding officer of the USS Hornet (CV-8) from October 1941 to July 1942; Commander Apollo Soucek, USN, Naval Aviator #3145, air officer; Commander George R. Henderson, USN, Naval Aviator #909, executive officer; Commander Frank Akers, USN, Naval Aviator #3228, navigator. From 1962 to 1963, Rear Admiral Akers was the Gray Eagle, the active duty aviator with the earliest designation as a naval aviator.
**For an account of the 1925 Schneider cup race, which Lieutenant Doolittle won in a Curtiss R3C-2 at a record speed of 232 miles per hour, see "Winning in the Turns," by Terry Gwynn-Jones (Air Force Magazine, January 1985, pages 84-87).

hear ye." And everybody aboard was told not exactly where we were going, not exactly what we were going to do, but that this was a mission against Japan. From then on, there was complete rapport. There was no--as a matter of fact, the Tokyo fliers were given the best of everything. If they were rooming with a chap, he gave him the best place in the room, the best bed. Captain Mitscher, as you say, gave me his quarters, because he said, "You will want to be holding meetings from time to time with either all of your people or some of them at a time, and consequently it would be more convenient for you to have a place where you can do that. My quarters makes that possible, and that's the only place on the ship," whereupon he moved into the smaller quarters himself and made his quarters our meeting place. So we could not have had better cooperation from then on. As I said, the boys felt a little out of place on a carrier, and the carrier people felt a little out of place, they felt they were a little out of place, but after that first "Hear ye, hear ye," there was complete and utter cooperation at every level.

I don't know whether any of the books said, but prior to Admiral Halsey leaving San Francisco in the <u>Enterprise</u>, he and I had met in a little restaurant where we had a table way back in the corner.* And we discussed the operation from every point of view. We tried to think of every contingency that might possibly

---
    *Vice Admiral William F. Halsey, Jr., USN, Commander Carriers Pacific and, at the time of the Doolittle Raid, Commander Task Force 16.

arise and have an answer to that contingency.

One of the things that we considered was being apprehended before we got to Japan. And the plan was that if we were within range of Japan, we would go ahead and bomb our targets, fly out to sea and hope, rather futilely, to be picked up by one of the two submarines that were in the area. If we were within range of the Hawaiian Islands--say, Midway--we would immediately clear their decks and proceed to Midway so they could utilize the task force properly.

If, on the other hand, we weren't within range of anyplace we could go, we would push our aircraft overboard so that the Hornet's deck would be cleared, and they could protect themselves. I believe that Admiral Halsey and I really sat down and considered every possible eventuality--one of which eventuated.

Q: And you did this over a good San Francisco dinner for about three hours or so.

General Doolittle: That's right.*

Q: You don't recall the name of the restaurant, do you, General?

General Doolittle: No. It was not a fashionable place; it was a little place where we could get back in the corner, unobserved.

Q: I see. It probably doesn't exist. When you were aboard the ship, did Captain Mitscher come down and take dinner with you occasionally, or did he stay up on the bridge all the time?

---

*Shortly after the end of World War II, Fleet Admiral Halsey dictated what amounted to an oral history. Concerning his meeting in San Francisco about the Tokyo raid, Halsey said:

"It immediately occurred to me that a personal contact with Jimmy Doolittle, whom I did not know at that time, was desirable. First, so that we could size each other up, and secondly, to discuss ways and means. Chester Nimitz agreed and gave me orders to proceed to the Alameda Naval Air Base via San Diego. Miles [Captain Miles Browning, Halsey's chief of staff] and I made the trip in a Navy plane and after completing our duty in San Diego, flew to San Francisco. In order to preserve the secrecy of our mission, we decided a meeting with Jimmy in Alameda was not desirable. We met in San Francisco at the Fairmont Hotel. Our first meeting place was at the bar of the Fairmont, but Jimmy had too many friends and we eventually moved to my room where we were not subject to interruption. The project was gone over and we came to an agreement as to ways and means."

While reviewing the transcript of this interview for release, General Doolittle was provided a copy of the Halsey recollection concerning the site of the meeting. General Doolittle agreed to defer to Halsey's version because it was recorded much closer in time to the event than was his own. The transcript of the Halsey oral history is on file at the Naval Historical Center in Washington, D.C.

General Doolittle: He stayed on the bridge most of the time, but he was always available if there was anything that we wanted to ask. He was 100% cooperative and in no way obstrusive.

Q: When Lieutenant Miller first introduced the technique for carrier takeoffs in a B-25, was it a bit of a shock to your land field aviators?

General Doolittle: Yes, it was, indeed, because the folks who had not had carrier takeoff training had all been taught never to pull the airplane off the ground until you had good flying speed.

Q: And what did you consider that--100 knots or so?

General Doolittle: Well, that was comfortably--hopefully--with enough maneuverability and enough excess speed to get someplace where you weren't going to crack up or else get where you would minimize the effects of crack-up. So the taking off in a stall is something that they had been taught not to do from the time they started flying. On the other hand, taking off in a stall is essential if you're going to get off a carrier with a heavy load. So it required a complete change in philosophical outlook and in technique. As I mentioned before, two of the boys, unfortunately, took off in a little too much of a stall and lost control of their airplane. Nobody hurt, luckily.

Q: You put the flaps down.

General Doolittle: We took off with full flaps on training, and took off with full flaps on taking off from the Hornet. One airplane inadvertently--when the chap put his flaps down, then went to put the flap lever in neutral, he apparently put it up about half an inch above neutral, and the flaps milked up.

Q: This is Lieutenant Lawson?

General Doolittle: Yes. And nobody noticed until he was on his way, and he took off with only partial flaps or none. And he went off the bow and settled. But by slamming his tail down again just before he hit the water, why, he was able to pull out. That was the only close call that occurred. There were other airplanes that took off inadvertently on the upbeat. They delayed a little or weren't quite in synchronization with the chap who waved them off, and there were a couple of those that sort of floated for a minute and then went on.

Q: While we're on this, I'll ask you--you took off first on this flight from the Hornet. Do you recall the sensation? Were you happy with your takeoff?

General Doolittle: I felt perfectly comfortable, because there was a 30-knot wind. I knew that had there been a dead calm we could have made about 30 knots, but as it was, there was about a 30-knot wind. In those heavy seas, the carrier was still making something over 20 knots, so we had over a 50-knot wind across the deck.

Q: And you could get off at 70?

General Doolittle: That was a lifesaver.

Q: And you could get off in 70 knots airspeed. So if you made 20 knots, then you would have been airborne. That's interesting. Well, I remember Hank Miller said you made a very fine takeoff and set the example for the others. I guess that except for Lieutenant Lawson they all were okay.

One of the things that we worry about these days on any operation is security. I think that the recent--at least the 1980 raid in Iran which we aborted and made from a carrier with the helicopters--criticism now is the operation was so secure and compartmented that it hindered the people making the operation.*

---

*On 24 April 1980, an operation was launched from the USS Nimitz (CVN-68) to rescue 53 Americans held hostage at the U.S. Embassy in Tehran. The mission was aborted when three of eight helicopters developed problems. Eight of the would-be rescuers were killed when a helicopter sliced into a transport plane on the ground. The complete story of the rescue attempt is in The Iranian Rescue Mission: Why it Failed by Captain Paul B. Ryan, USN(Ret.), (Annapolis, Maryland: Naval Institute Press, 1985).

In your case, you had pretty good security, but you didn't have any problems with compartmentation or anything.

General Doolittle: See, we were isolated. After we got on the carrier, it was complete isolation.

Q: True, true.

General Doolittle: There was one little thing that really shocked me. My wife was in San Francisco just before we took off. As we were going upstairs in the elevator at the hotel, some young chap got on and said, "Hey, I understand you're taking off tomorrow morning." I mumbled something, but for a minute I was terribly shocked, and it was apparently a complete coincidence, that we had put out a cover story so that when the Hornet was seen with the airplanes aboard her, which had to be seen going under Golden Gate Bridge--you couldn't avoid it. The cover story was that these airplanes were being taken to Honolulu where we needed them very quickly.

Q: Perfectly logical.

General Doolittle: Why we didn't fly them there wasn't said.

Q: Well, that's perfectly logical. Every ship carried aircraft.

The carriers did on the deck. Did you sense that some of your people who were working on this project eventually--into January, February, maybe even March--finally put pieces together and knew what was going on?

General Doolittle: They knew that we were going to bomb Japan. They couldn't help but know that we were going to be on a carrier or we wouldn't be practicing carrier takeoffs. But other than that, they had no specific instructions until they got on the carrier and were briefed. Each one was briefed on a selected target, and they were told that the mission was an important mission. They were told that any leak would jeopardize the success of the mission and jeopardize their lives. So, as far as I know, there were no leaks even though the boys had their families there, many of them, at Eglin Field. Quite a few of the boys had their families there.

Q: General, some time in February you wrote a paper for General Arnold outlining the plan. One of the paragraphs that you included was "Lieutenant Colonel Doolittle will be in charge of and in personal command of the operation." This put it right up to General Arnold as to make a decision one way or the other. In other words, you faced him with this. Did he concur? Is that the time he called you in and said, "No, I want you on my staff"?

General Doolittle: He never was enthusiastic about me commanding the thing. It was a flattering thing that he wanted me on his staff. I believe you read in one of the books that when I asked him for permission to lead the mission, he first said, "No." And then when he saw the disappointment on my face, he said, "Well, I have no objection unless Miff has an objection." Miff Harmon was his chief of staff.

Q: That's General Harmon.*

General Doolittle: General Harmon. So I thanked him and then ran as fast as I could run around to Miff Harmon's office. When I got in to see General Harmon, I said, "General Arnold has no objection to me leading this mission if you don't." Now, remember, this is minutes--not much more than seconds--after he had told me I could lead it.

Q: This is the old Munitions Building?

General Doolittle: Yes. So Harmon said, "I have no objections, Jimmy."

I said, "Thank you very much, sir," and turned around, saluted him, and started out. Then as I got outside, I ran as fast as I could run about three or four doors down to Hap

---
*Major General Millard F. Harmon, USA.

Arnold's office--to Miff Harmon's office. And so when he said he had no objections, if I hadn't run out of there as fast as I could run, why, I wouldn't have made it.

Q: Yes, I understand.

General Doolittle: Because just as I walked out the door, I heard the squawk box on. I heard Miff Harmon saying, "But Hap, I just told him he could go."

Q: I get the picture all right, sir. Back in the second of February of 1942, the Hornet, newly commissioned, was at Norfolk, and one day they came in from exercises out in the Chesapeake Bay and were told to take on board two B-25s with Army pilots and to go out and launch them and come back in. Lieutenant McCarthy and Lieutenant Fitzgerald were the two Army pilots.* Did you have a hand in this?

General Doolittle: I think it was a good thing to do. They took off with a light load and showed that it was possible to at least get off with a light load. The only other problem was the problem of taking off with a much heavier load.

---

*Lieutenant James F. McCarthy, USA; Lieutenant John E. Fitzgerald, USA.

Q: Yes, that was the first time, I gather, that a multi-engine aircraft had done this.

General Doolittle: As far as I know. Certainly the first time that B-25s had.

Q: Yes. In this connection, the North African operation was coming up. Did General Arnold ever discuss with you a plan of flying B-25s off a carrier for the North African...

General Doolittle: No, I didn't know anything about that until I read your notes.

Q: I checked the literature on this, and I couldn't find anything on it, either.

General Doolittle: I did know that they had talked about flying some of the fighters aboard.

Q: P-40s?

General Doolittle: Off. And just what happened with that, I don't know. I think they were all brought in boxes, were they not?

Q: That's my understanding. Yes, sir.

General Doolittle: My recollection is dim on it, but I do remember that there was talk of flying the fighters off the carriers, and they, I believe, did not do so. That might have gotten mixed up with the bombers.

Q: After the training period at Eglin Field, I understand that Lieutenant Miller asked your permission to go along to the West Coast, and you had previously thought that perhaps you could find somebody on the West Coast to take his place. He evidently said it was a matter of personal pride with him or professional pride to go along to the West Coast at least.

General Doolittle: We were delighted to have him.

Q: You were? My. He also said that the 16th B-25 was put on board with the intention of letting him demonstrate a takeoff and fly back to Columbia, South Carolina, return it to the Army Air Corps, and go back to Pensacola.

General Doolittle: Yes.

Q: And when he got on board, everything was nicely spaced.

General Doolittle: When he got on board, things looked so good, the airplanes looked so good, there was no crowding of airplanes. Captain Mitscher and I got our heads together, and we both agreed that it would be better to have one more airplane on the raid than to have one airplane sent home. So we made the decision that that airplane would stay on.

Q: I don't think that Lieutenant Miller had much luggage with him, though.

General Doolittle: No.

Q: Did you ever receive a briefing from Captain Duncan on the whole operation? He had a handwritten operation order or plan, and as I understand it, he showed it to you, and you read it once and completely agreed and said, "That's fine," and that's the only order that ever was written.

General Doolittle: As far as I know.

Q: So you operated without any written op order?

General Doolittle: No. Hap Arnold really gave me complete control of the Army end of the thing and did not interfere in any way, except that he almost took me off, almost didn't let me go.

Q: I see.

General Doolittle: But that was very flattering because he felt that I could do more good as one of his troubleshooters. You see, I had a rather unique advantage in that I was an aeronautical engineer, and I had been a test pilot and had flown a great deal. And there were lots of problems. One of the problems was the B-26. The B-26 was a good airplane, but it had some tricks. And so he gave--one of the first jobs that I got when I went on his staff in Washington--was to recommend whether we should continue to build the B-26 or whether we should cancel all B-26 contracts. Well, I immediately got the B-26, practiced with it, and came to the conclusion that it was an excellent airplane. It had some characteristics that were unique and that what we needed was an intermediate plane that was somewhat harder to fly than the then advanced trainer. That is, the primary trainer, then the advanced trainer, and then the B-26 was too big a step. There had to be something in it. Well, that was done. The B-26 continued to be produced and proved itself to be a very good airplane. They did, in the due course of time, put a little bigger wings on. But that was the sort of job that I was doing for Hap Arnold. Knowing industry, having been a part of industry, half my life in the industry, half active life, half in the military, I gave him a particular brand of knowledge that was very helpful to him.

Q: Yes, sir.

General Doolittle: That's why he didn't want to let me go.

Q: The joint Army-Navy Board, back in the late Thirties, as I understand it, had made an agreement that on any joint operation that the Navy would deliver the Army to the water line, and then they were on their own. But as long as the Army was on board the ship, then the Navy had command.

General Doolittle: That's right.

Q: And this was, without anybody saying so, I'm sure this was the assumption you made.

General Doolittle: No, as far as I know, there wasn't a speck of misunderstanding and certainly not a speck of discord.

Q: I wouldn't think there would be, since after your meeting with Admiral Halsey, it was all laid on.

General Doolittle: We laid everything on, and our relationship with Captain Mitscher was, I thought, first class.

Q: Later on, General, did people ever come up to you and say, "You know, I suggested the idea of this raid back in 1939," or "I did it in 1940," or "I spoke to General Arnold, and he picked the idea up"? Did you ever run into that or not?

General Doolittle: Not that specifically, but undoubtedly other people had thought of it. Then when it was actually accomplished, why, they would immediately say, yes, that they had thought of it.

Q: Well, I'm sure the general idea . . .

General Doolittle: It came as a complete surprise to me, and I'm pretty sure it came as a complete surprise to General Arnold.

Q: Yes, sir. General, your navigators were used to navigating on land, and I recall an old expression of navigators in aircraft following the railway tracks as a means of getting from one place to another. Did your navigators on the 16 B-25s need some brushing up?

General Doolittle: Yes, they all got brushing up on the carrier. They were all competent to use a sextant. However, it was very seldom used over land. We usually had enough landmarks--either visual or electronic--to not really need the sextant. So their brush-up in navigation while on the Hornet was very valuable.

Q: At the time you left San Francisco, a Navy blimp came out and lowered some bubble windows for the aircraft in order that the navigators could shoot the stars. It was later determined that you didn't need these; that you used the plexiglas window. Is that correct, sir?

General Doolittle: As I remember it. That's a detail that I'm not sure of. I don't remember any problems.

Q: General, when the B-25s were hoisted aboard, they were spotted on the flight deck, and all the shipboard aircraft were brought down to the hangar deck and some of them lashed up to the overhead. Your B-25s took up the latter part of the flight deck and were subjected to strong winds, I imagine, on this cruise to the 600-mile circle off Tokyo. Did you have any maintenance problems?

General Doolittle: Yes, we had some leaky tanks. We ran up the engines periodically, though, in order to make sure that everything was all right. We had some of our own mechanics aboard, but the Navy was most helpful. I believe we had to change an engine.

Q: Yes, sir. They actually built a small canvas tent over the engine on deck.

General Doolittle: But as far as I know, there was just--and I should know if anything was wrong, and there wasn't anything wrong. There was just a complete cooperation between the carrier's mechanics and our mechanics as you could possibly ask for. Now, there was one very untoward thing that happened at the depot in Sacramento. We had all of our engines adjusted by a Stromberg carburetor man, all our carburetors adjusted--not according to regulations, but in order to get maximum range, accepting some little difficulty in starting, accepting all of the compromises that you make when you get something that can't go wrong. And so when we got there, I left word that we wanted the airplanes completely checked but not to touch the carburetor setting, which was what we needed, and under no consideration change them. The second day there, I was down and found an engine backfiring. I went to see what the hell was the matter. I was madder than a son of a bitch, so I said to the mechanic--a civilian mechanic was running the airplane--"What's going on here?"

He said, "We're just readjusting the carburetors. They're all out of adjustment." Well, I naturally blew my top. But that cost us quite a bit of range, because we never had a chance again to have them set back to the proper long-range setting and recheck it.

Q: Yes, I recall Captain York suffered excessive fuel consumption. Was he the one that went into Russia?*

General Doolittle: He went to Russia against orders.

Q: General, were you satisfied with the weather reports you were getting for planning the flight? I mean, while you were on board the ship, did you get fairly good predictions?

General Doolittle: We had fairly good predictions, yes. We had very good predictions.

Q: As I understand it from Lieutenant Cumberledge, who is now a captain retired, he got weather data from Pearl Harbor, Alaska, and the West Coast, and put together his weather map on that basis.** You had a cold front, as I understand it, going toward Japan, and then you had bad weather going all the way to Japan. Is that correct?

General Doolittle: Well, what happened was that we had quite a

---
*Captain Edward J. York, USA, pilot of crew #8, ran low of fuel and had to choose between ditching 300 miles into the China Sea or landing in the Soviet Union, where Stalin had already refused to participate in the raid. York chose the latter, resulting in a 13-month internment in Russia.
**Lieutenant Arthur A. Cumberledge, USN.

sea when we launched. Then there was overcast until we got almost to Japan. And when we got almost to Japan, the weather cleared up. That was the time when we would have liked to have been obscured a little bit. Then when we left Japan, we found that we had a pretty strong head wind, and we got, I guess, halfway to China before the wind abated and then turned around and gave us a tail wind for the rest of the way in. So we were flying under the weather, so it didn't make any difference until we got to China. When we got to China, then we had to pull up into the weather because the clouds were on the hills.

Q: You didn't want to run into a hill.

General Doolittle: That's right, and by that time it was dark.

Q: And so of the 80 men in the 16 aircraft, 71 survived the mission.

General Doolittle: One was killed when he jumped in his parachute. Two were drowned when they landed off the shore of China in the water. Eight were taken prisoner by the Japanese, and of those eight, three were executed, and one died of beri-beri and malnutrition in a Japanese prison.

Q: Yes, sir. On the 16th of April, General, Reuters British

Doolittle - 35

News Agency broadcast a report that three U.S. bombers had hit Tokyo. This was an amazing coincidence in the light of what happened two days later. Did you ever find out how this report got through?

General Doolittle: No.

Q: When you ran into the Japanese picket boats early in the morning of 18 April, you must have sensed then that you'd have to modify your plan and take off earlier than you had anticipated. Did this strike you?

General Doolittle: We immediately ran into the picket boats. We started preparations for leaving the area then.

Q: I see. I see. Did Admiral Halsey communicate this thought to you, and you both agreed that this was the way to go?

General Doolittle: No. We had the complete understanding as to what we would do.

Q: No discussion?

General Doolittle: Nothing. No decision to be made. Just go

ahead with plans. We had to get off there as quickly as possible and on with the show so that he could turn around and withdraw at all possible speed.

Q: Do you recall the actual conditions just the morning at 0800 when you took off? Was there a sun out, or was it cloudy? How did it look?

General Doolittle: It was cloudy.

Q: And heavy seas.

General Doolittle: Fairly limited overcast.

Q: Not ideal weather by any means for takeoff.

General Doolittle: No, a storm blowing up, as a matter of fact--high seas.

Q: After the raid, General, when you returned to Washington, were you called in to the White House?

General Doolittle: Well, what happened--immediately I returned, I was put under cover so that the press wouldn't find me. The story--what was it?

Q: Shangri-la.

General Doolittle: The Shangri-la story would be brought out again.* On one occasion I was told to be ready at a certain time, and I was picked up, and in the car with me were General Arnold and General Marshall. We started out in a complete silence, and finally I said, "Well, now, I'm not too sharp. If you were to tell me what this is all about, I'm sure I could comport myself better." I saw them look at each other.

General Marshall said, "We are going to the White House, where the President will give you the Medal of Honor." I didn't say anything. He said, "Well, you don't seem very pleased."

I said, "Well, I don't think I earned the Medal of Honor. The Medal of Honor, to me, was something that was given where one chap lost his own life saving somebody else's life. So I don't think I earned it."

General Marshall said--it's the only time he ever spoke sternly to me--he said, "I think you earned it."

I said, "Yes, sir."**

Q: I can see him doing that, too. What happened when you got to the White House?

---

*Two days after the Doolittle Raid, the U.S. War Department issued a report describing the action, but not disclosing its origination point. President Franklin Roosevelt remarked that the pilots had taken off from Shangri-la, the fictional paradise in James Hilton's 1933 novel Lost Horizon.
**Doolittle, by then promoted to brigadier general, was awarded the Medal of Honor on 9 June 1942.

General Doolittle: We got to the White House, and we had to wait a very short time for our turn to see the President, and then were taken in to the President. Oh, in the meantime, they had picked up my wife. And so it was General Arnold, General Marshall, my wife, and myself. The President hung the medal on me and said a few appropriate words, which I've forgotten.

Q: Did the President stand up to do this?

General Doolittle: No, he did it sitting down.

Q: And you leaned over, then, I gather. Who else was present besides General Marshall and General Arnold?

General Doolittle: I don't remember anyone else being present. I don't know why.

Q: The Secretary of War Stimson, maybe?[*]

General Doolittle: I don't believe so.

Q: Well, it was still hush-hush.

---

[*]Henry L. Stimson, Secretary of War from 1940 to 1945.

General Doolittle: I'm almost sure that we were five there. General Arnold, General Marshall, my wife and myself, and the President. They did have a photographer come in and take some pictures.

Q: One of the young officers on the Hornet was Ensign Richard Laning, who later became a nuclear submarine commander.* And he was the--I guess we'd call it the radar officer now. They did have an SC radar on board. And he tells me that they talked about some sort of an instrument on board your B-25 to detect Japanese radar, and he rigged up a portable VHF transceiver with a whip antenna detecting Japanese radar, and he tested it against the Enterprise radar. When you learned of this, you asked if he would like to go along to operate this gear, and they actually drilled a hole with a whip antenna in the B-25 and put in a canvas seat. But the idea was that if the B-25 got within close, that Laning would go, but if they didn't get in close, he would not go. So he didn't. Do you recall this incident?

General Doolittle: I don't remember it.

Q: Well, it's one of those minor things.

---

*Ensign Richard B. Laning, USN, served in USS Hornet (CV-8) from October 1941 to August 1942. He later commanded the second nuclear-powered submarine, USS Seawolf (SSN-575) from March 1957 to December 1958. Captain Laning has been interviewed for a Naval Institute oral history.

Doolittle - 40

General Doolittle: It's a long time ago, and it's a detail. I don't remember it.

Q: When you were in Captain Mitscher's mess, did you take your meals alone, General, or did you eat with your squadron commander?

General Doolittle: I ate with my gang.

Q: I see. And these are the senior officers of the group. All 16 officers?

General Doolittle: Yes.

Q: I see. Well, that certainly made for a unity of purpose right there. Also, I wanted to ask since the Hornet mechs seemed to be familiar with your engines, what type engine did the B-25 have? It's a long way back.

General Doolittle: It had a Wright 2600.

Q: Wright 2600.

General Doolittle: Fourteen-cylinder engine, if I remember. No, wait a minute. Yes, I guess 14 cylinder.

Q: How much horsepower did it produce? Six-hundred or 700?

General Doolittle: I've forgotten.

Q: I was curious to know if possibly the carrier aircraft used the same type engine which you had.

General Doolittle: It was an engine used by both the Army and the Navy.

Q: General, looking back on the operation, with regard to its military features--and I'm talking about the principles of war-- could you comment on why you think it was a success?

General Doolittle: I think what contributed to its success more than anything else was teamwork, complete cooperation between the Army and the Navy. Today I think we probably have better cooperation between the services than at any time in my lifetime. There has always, in the past, been insufficient money, insufficient material, insufficient people--number of people--to go around. And the services have always endeavored to do their job as best they could, and that meant getting as much of the material, equipment, and as many of the people as they could. This has caused some discord in the past between the services. I don't think that will ever be completely overcome. I think there will always be at least healthy service rivalry. But when people begin to think more of service than of country, then we get into a bad situation. And I think today the military services are working more closely together making do, as they must, with not enough, really, for anybody--certainly not enough for everybody--better than we ever have before. And I think that is the healthiest thing in the United States of America today.

Q: General, back in 1925, you won the Schneider Cup Seaplane Race in a Navy Curtiss R3C-2 aircraft. How did you acquire this Navy plane?

General Doolittle: You're going back to a time when there was less for the military than there is today, and we don't feel--those of us who have had some military experience--that the military is getting what it needs to do a job today, although it is coming closer to it than it has for quite a while. And so it was decided between the Army and the Navy that they would buy four racing airplanes from the Curtiss Company. The total bill for those four airplanes, complete with engines and spare parts, was a half a million dollars. And that was very difficult to come by. One of those four airplanes was tested to destruction in order to find out--statically tested to destruction--in order to find out whether they were sound. Of the other three, two went to the Navy and one went to the Army. These airplanes were to be used with pontoons in order to fly in the Schneider Trophy Race. Exactly the same airplanes with the pontoons off and wheels put on in place were to fly in the Pulitzer Race.* I was selected to be the chap who flew the seaplane, the Army chap that flew the seaplane. Cy Bettis was selected to be the Army chap who flew the Army plane in the Pulitzer Race. Al Williams was Navy test pilot on the airplane. I was Army test pilot on the airplane. I had the advantage over the other folks of considerable technical training and was able to make modifications, for instance, in the propeller pitch setting, that made the Army plane a little faster than the two Navy planes. Al Williams flew the Pulitzer, and Cy Bettis flying the Army plane beat him. I flew in the Schneider and had the fastest plane in the Schneider Trophy Race. So that is the story of $500,000, which seemed a tremendous fortune.

Q: Yes, it was. Back in 1928, General, Captain Emory Land, U.S. Navy, arranged for two-year leave from the Army for you to develop instrument flight at Mitchel Field.** Is this correct, sir?

---

*In the 1925 Pulitzer Race, flown on 10 October, Army Lieutenant Cyrus Bettis beat Navy Lieutenant Alford J. Williams at a speed of almost 249 miles per hour, both flying R3C-1s. Sixteen days later, Lieutenant Doolittle won the Schneider Trophy in Lieutenant Bettis's plane, now equipped with pontoons and redesignated R3C-2.

**During World War II, Vice Admiral Land, cousin of famed aviator Charles A. Lindbergh, headed the administration of merchant shipping.

General Doolittle: That is correct. Captain Land (later Vice Admiral Land) was loaned to Harry Guggenheim, and Harry Guggenheim wanted to do several things.* One was to have a safe airplane competition. In those days, a lot of people were being killed by getting an airplane in a spin and not knowing how to get it out. And it became known as the deadly spin, tailspin. Harry Guggenheim offered a prize--a substantial prize--for an airplane that couldn't be spun--no matter what you did, you couldn't make it spin. That competition was won by the Curtiss Company with an airplane called the Curtiss Tanager. Oddly enough, Handley-Page also had an airplane in that competition, and he was pretty upset because the Tanager won because it had Handley-Page slots, flap slots.

But simultaneously with that--or perhaps just a little ahead of it--Harry Guggenheim conceived the idea of the developing of instruments and techniques that would permit airplanes to fly regardless of weather. For all of this, as his military advisor and as his right hand, he had borrowed Captain Jerry Land from the Navy. Later-Admiral Land was running all of these things for Harry Guggenheim.

Q: Captain Land was assistant chief of the Bureau of

---

*Harry F. Guggenheim, naval aviator #1129, was the son of Daniel Guggenheim, who established the Guggenheim Fund for the Promotion of Aeronautics in 1926 with a $2.5 million grant. Harry, a World War I aviator, served as the fund's president.

Aeronautics, I believe, at the time.

General Doolittle: For a while he was spending a great deal of his time with Harry Guggenheim.

Q: This is the Guggenheim Foundation family?

General Doolittle: Yes, and Guggenheim Fund.

Q: Right.

General Doolittle: That was the Guggenheim Fund for the Promotion of Aeronautics, and these were the two principal projects.

Q: I see.

General Doolittle: Captain Land had an office in New York with the Guggenheims. He spent a great deal of his time. When he was asked who was the best chap to run the flight test laboratory, or blind-flying laboratory, he endeared himself to the Army and earned the Navy's emnity by naming me.

Q: Did you know him?

General Doolittle: No, I didn't know him.

Q: You didn't know Captain Land?

General Doolittle: At that time--when that decision was made, I might have met him, but I didn't know him at all well. I came to know him very well. I admired him profoundly. But he was in bad repute with the Navy for a while because he had chosen an Army pilot instead of a Navy, and when asked why, he said, "This chap has the advantage over any of our Navy people of not only a lifetime of flying, but a technical education that has given him a distinct advantage in the development of new equipment." And so from then on, I came to know him and admired him. We became hunting companions. He loved to hunt, I loved to hunt. And Harry Guggenheim had the Cane Hoy Plantation out in Charleston, South Carolina. He invited Jerry and me and several other folks every year to come down and shoot turkeys and quail. And so I loved--as one man could love another man, I loved Jerry. He was just a wonderful, wonderful man.

Q: Going back seven years before that, General, you took part in the bombing of old warships, old German warships in Chesapeake Bay in 1921. Did you have any contact with naval officers at that time?

General Doolittle: No, none whatsoever. I had contact with naval officers in 1925 when I was trained in seaplanes but not during the '21 bombing maneuvers.

Q: Was this at Anacostia Naval Air Station where you learned to fly seaplanes?

General Doolittle: Anacostia, yes.

Q: Do you recall your instructor?

General Doolittle: No, I don't.

Q: Or you had several. And you checked out, probably, in a couple of hours, I imagine, did you not?

General Doolittle: It wasn't too much of a chore to transfer from land planes to seaplanes.

Q: Yes, sir. Back in 1921, did you participate in dropping these huge 1,000-, 2,000-pound bombs on the Ostfriesland?*

---

*The German battleship Ostfriesland was taken by the U.S. Navy at the end of World War I, and commissioned in April 1920. This ship, and several other ex-German warships, were used as air targets by Army planes from Langley Field, Virginia. She was finally sunk on 21 July 1921 off the Virginia Capes.

General Doolittle: That operation was broken up into two basic types of planes. One were the Martin bombers, twin-engine Martin bombers that flew and dropped the larger bombs that sank the Ostfriesland. I was assigned to a DH outfit that dropped 100-pound bombs, and we did bomb submarines and destroyers.

Q: I see.

General Doolittle: We did not take part in the--I did not personally take part in the bombing of the Ostfriesland.

Q: General, back in November 1945, there was a story in The New York Times where you had taken issue with Admiral Mitscher and the Navy over the publicity which was really a dispute between the Navy and the Air Force, where the Navy had praised the role of sea power as being the major force in winning the Pacific war, and you had brought out the fact that the B-29s had had a very important role, and the B-29 pilots who were dead would sleep uneasily.* Do you want to comment on that dispute?

General Doolittle: Well, I did comment earlier on it indirectly.

---

*Articles appeared on the front page of The New York Times on 10 and 13 November 1945 after General Doolittle testified before the Senate Military Affairs Committee. In the first article it was noted that in response to comments by Admirals Nimitz and Mitscher claiming carrier air power had caused the Japanese to surrender, the general felt that joint teamwork accomplished the job.

The real problem has always been in getting what each service needs in order to do its job as well as it can possibly do it. There has never, even in time of war, been enough money to get enough equipment to satisfy the services' desires, because with more equipment and more people, they felt they could do their job better. So there were honest differences of opinion. And sometimes they came almost to the point of being acrimonious. And then I mentioned earlier--and would like to reiterate--that today these services do not have what they need, what they would like to have in order to do their jobs as well as they possibly could. We don't have the spare parts, we don't have the supplies, we don't have the equipment that we would like to have--the spare parts, the supplies, the back-up like fuel. These things are in short supply. And our staying power in a conventional war would be determined by the supplies that we have. I noticed in the paper yesterday, they said that the great fuel supply hole that's dug in the ground down here--they have put only enough fuel in to test it and see that it doesn't leak. But if we were to have a protracted war, the necessity for a stockpile of fuel is absolutely essential. It's obvious. And still the decision was made not to put any fuel in there yet. And so these are the things that have made it difficult for the services and made the services sometimes less than completely cooperative with each other.

Then I reiterate that today I think despite the fact that our economy and our military are in direct conflict for the few dollars that are available, there not being enough for both, both have to make some compromises. But the services, in my mind, are working more closely together today than they ever have in my lifetime.

Q: General, after this flare-up in 1945, did you and Admiral Mitscher ever meet again?

General Doolittle: I don't remember meeting him again. I can't say that categorically, because my memory's gotten very flabby.

Q: I don't agree with that, sir, but . . .

General Doolittle: It's odd that some things imprint themselves indelibly on your memory, and other things that are probably frequently much more important you can't recall to save your soul.

Q: I have one last question here. From what you've already said, I know the answer. But I'll phrase it anyway. The Chief of Naval Operations and the Chief of Staff of Air Force operate today with an agreement on joint efforts to enhance U.S. Air Force contributions to maritime operations. Now, this may involve cross-training and joint use of weapon schools and integration of forces on maneuvers. As a long-time Air Force pilot and as an honorary naval aviator, how do you view this step?

General Doolittle: I think it's very healthy and essential. We don't have what we need. Therefore, we must use what we have as effectively as possible. This helps achieve that objective.

Q: Well, thank you, General, for a very informative and interesting interview. I'm sure that historians of the future will look at your words very closely.

General, back in August 1945, when you stood on the deck of the battleship <u>Missouri</u> during the surrender ceremony, are there any thoughts that come back to you that you want to share with us?

General Doolittle: It was a very interesting experience, doubly interesting to me because I stood between two great generals--General Patton, General Simpson--both of whom I admired greatly.*
And the unique thing--that this whole thing was done without really any formality. We were all practically in fatigues. I remember on Okinawa when I found that I was to go up to Tokyo, I immediately got my blouse out. I found it had been in the foot

---

*General George S. Patton, Jr., USA, Commander U.S. 7th Army at the time of the Japanese surrender; General William H. Simpson, USA, Commander U.S. 9th Army.

locker all the time I had been in Okinawa. It was moldy and in terrible shape, and I didn't see how in the world I was going to get that blouse straightened out in order to wear it at a formal affair. I had a little house boy who was going to help me, and so I had him brush the blouse, brush the mold off, and then press it. I told him to be very careful in pressing it and use a damp cloth so as not to burn it. He apparently forgot and left the iron on, and when I finally noticed what was going on, it was obviously impossible to get that uniform into a shape where I could wear it. So I was just delighted when word came at the last minute that we were going to dress very informally. And it was a very interesting experience.

Q: Did you meet your old wartime friends in the Navy at this affair, also? Most of them were there, I imagine.

General Doolittle: There wasn't the amount of moving around and meeting friends that we would liked to have had. The thing was-- while it was in informal dress, the whole thing was pretty formal, and you marched in and marched out.

Q: You saw Admiral Halsey many times later, I suppose?

General Doolittle: Probably the most interesting session I had with Admiral Halsey was a year or two after the war was over--I guess two years after the war was over. We were both living in New York, and at that time Australia felt very kindly toward us, and each year they had the Coral Sea ceremony, where the Battle of the Coral Sea saved Australia.* They were very, very happy. So each year they had a Coral Sea ceremony. It didn't last a day like our Fourth of July; it lasted a week. And one of the first people to be invited over to represent the United States was Admiral Halsey. He came back, and the first thing I knew, I was invited to go over to be the United States representative in order to have an airman. So I went immediately to Admiral Halsey and asked if he would brief me on what went on. He very kindly did, and that was the last time that I really had a long session with him. I was and am one of his sincere fans.

Q: Thank you, General.

---

*The Battle of the Coral Sea, 7-8 May 1942, was a tactical standoff, but it thwarted Japan's intention of invading Australia and using that nation to strategic advantage.

Index

to

Reminiscences of

General James H. Doolittle

U.S. Air Force (Retired)

Air Force, U.S.
    Doolittle's thoughts on joint Navy-Air Force training and missions, pages 50-51

Anacostia Naval Air Station
    Doolittle learned to fly seaplanes here in mid-Twenties, page 47

Arnold, Lieutenant General Henry H., USA (USMA, 1907)
    Approached Doolittle with idea for Tokyo raid in January 1942, page 1; discussed arrangements with Doolittle, pages 2-4; initially refused Doolittle permission to lead raid, pages 4, 22-24, 27; gave Doolittle complete control in running projected raid, pages 11, 27; had staff officer Doolittle assess B-26 bomber, pages 28-29; accompanied Doolittle to White House for Medal of Honor in June 1942, pages 37-39

Australia
    Doolittle invited to Coral Sea celebrations after the war, pages 52-53

B-25 Bombers
    Planes used in April 1942 Doolittle raid on Japan modified beforehand, pages 8, 31-32; two planes lost in training for raid, pages 11-12, 18; training in carrier takeoffs, pages 18-19; two planes practiced with carrier in February 1942, pages 24-25; maintenance of planes on Hornet (CV-8), page 31; discussion of engine, pages 40-41

B-26 Bomber
    As an aeronautical engineer, Doolittle was in a position to assess this plane for General Hap Arnold during World War II, page 28

Bettis, Lieutenant Cyrus, USA
    Won the 1925 Pulitzer Race in a modified Curtiss seaplane, page 43

Bombing Practice
    On ex-German warships after World War I, pages 46-48

Boxing
    Beneficial to Doolittle in flying, pages 10-11

Chiang Kai-shek
    Wary of Japanese reaction to any Chinese help with Doolittle raid, page 2

China
    Difficulty getting permission for planes from Doolittle raid to land in China, page 2; poor weather around Chinese coast after raid, page 34

Coral Sea Ceremony
  After the war, Doolittle invited to Australia as U.S. representative to a remembrance celebration for the Battle of Coral Sea, pages 52-53

Cumberledge, Lieutenant Arthur A., USN (1931)
  Responsible for weather maps used for planning Tokyo raid, page 33

Curtiss Company
  Seaplanes acquired by the Army and Navy from Curtiss in the early Twenties, page 42; Curtiss Tanager won substantial prize from Guggenheim Fund as spin-resistant airplane, page 44

Doolittle, General James H., USAF
  Approached with idea for raid in January 1942, pages 1-3; initially was refused permission to lead raid, page 4; in on planning raid, pages 4,7; felt comfortable with carrier takeoffs, pages 19-20; wife, pages 21, 38-39; presented Medal of Honor on 9 June 1942, pages 37-39; attended Japanese surrender ceremony, pages 51-52; invited to Australia for Coral Sea celebration, pages 52-53

Doolittle Raid
  Background of idea for Tokyo air raid, page 1; preliminary planning, pages 2-3, 7; targeting, pages 3-5; dead reckoning used to reach Japan, pages 6, 30-31; reasons for not flying in formation, page 6; important psychological boost as offensive vs. defensive measure, pages 6-7; annual reunions held by those involved in raid, page 10; training of plane crews, pages 11-12, 18-19, 24; treatment of Army crews in <u>Hornet</u> (CV-8), pages 14-15; contingency plans discussed with Halsey in San Francisco, pages 15-17, 35; secrecy before departing, pages 20-22; briefing of crews, page 22; Army-Navy accord, pages 29, 31-32, 41; weather, pages 31, 33-34, 36; casualties, page 34; "Shangri-la" story, pages 36-37; <u>See</u> B-25 Bombers; 17th Bombardment Group

Duncan, Captain Donald B., USN (USNA, 1917)
  In charge of preliminary planning for Doolittle raid, pages 2-3, 7, 27

Eglin Field, Florida
  Army pilots trained at this Army Air Forces bases in early 1942 for Tokyo raid, pages 8, 13, 22, 26

Fitzgerald, Lieutenant John E., USA
  Flew B-25 off <u>Hornet</u> (CV-8) in February 1942 as preliminary test for Doolittle raid, page 24

Germany
  Bombing of Buckingham Palace during World War II steeled Britain against Germany, page 5; German battleships used for target practice after World War I, pages 46-48

Guggenheim, Harry F.
  Offered prize in late Twenties to aircraft designer who could come up with a plane that wouldn't spin, page 44; interested in developing instrument flying, pages 44-45

Gymnastics
  Doolittle considers tumbling experience was beneficial to his ability as a pilot, page 10

Halsey, Vice Admiral William F., Jr., USN (USNA, 1904)
  Met with Doolittle in San Francisco in early 1942 to discuss operation prior to Tokyo raid, pages 15-17, 29; after the war, briefed Doolittle on Australian Coral Sea ceremonies, pages 52-53

Handley-Page
  Aircraft manufacturer lost out on prize money for a spin-resistant plane in the late Twenties to an aircraft using Handley-Page slots, page 44

Harmon, Major General Millard F., USA (USMA, 1912)
  General Arnold's chief of staff, Harmon approved Doolittle's request to lead Tokyo raid, pages 23-24

Hornet, USS (CV-8)
  Involvement in Doolittle raid, pages 3, 12, 19; initial coolness by Navy personnel in Hornet towards Army airmen, pages 14-15; exercise with Army planes in February 1942, page 24; situation on deck with larger Army planes, pages 27, 31

Instrument Flying
  Doolittle in on development of this technique in the late Twenties, pages 43-46

Japan
  Targeting for April 1942 air raid, pages 3-4; eight Americans taken prisoner after raid, page 34; Doolittle's recollections of Japanese surrender ceremony, pages 51-52

Jones, Captain David M., USA
  Doolittle raid pilot was helpful in obtaining target folders and maps prior to flight, page 3

Jurika, Captain Stephen, Jr., USN (Ret.) (USNA, 1933)
  Briefed Doolittle on desirable Japanese targets, page 3

King, Admiral Ernest J., USN   (USNA, 1901)
   Approached with idea of Tokyo raid in January 1942, page 1; in on planning of raid, pages 2, 7, 9

Land, Captain Emory, USN   (USNA, 1902)
   Arranged for Doolittle to work on the development of instrument flying in the late Twenties, pages 43-46; assessed by Doolittle, page 46

Laning, Ensign Richard B., USN   (USNA, 1940)
   Stood available to assist in detecting Japanese radar before Doolittle raid, page 39

Low, Captain Francis S., USN   (USNA, 1915)
   Originated idea of Tokyo raid in January 1942, page 1

Marshall, General George C., USA
   First presented with idea for Doolittle raid in January 1942, page 1; accompanied Doolittle to White House for Medal of Honor in June 1942, pages 37-39

McCarthy, Lieutenant James F., USA
   Flew B-25 off of Hornet (CV-8) in February 1942 as preliminary test for Doolittle raid, page 24

Miller, Lieutenant Henry L, USN   (USNA, 1934)
   Friendship with Doolittle, pages 9-10; introduced technique for carrier takeoff in B-25, page 18; assessment of Doolittle's takeoff, page 20; accompanied Army pilots to West Coast to continue training, page 26

Missouri, USS (BB-63)
   Doolittle's recollections of Japanese surrender in September 1945, pages 51-52

Mitscher, Captain Marc A., USN   (USNA, 1910)
   As skipper of Hornet (CV-8) in April 1942, involvement with Doolittle and Army pilots, pages 13, 17-18, 27, 29; gave up his quarters to Doolittle, pages 14-15; Doolittle took issue with Mitscher's late-1945 claim that carrier air power had won the war, page 48

Ostfriesland
   Doolittle participated in target bombing on this ex-German battleship in the early Twenties, pages 47-48

Pulitzer Race
   Curtiss seaplane, modified with wheels instead of pontoons, entered in this race in October 1925, page 43

R3C-1
  Curtiss seaplane, modified with wheels instead of pontoons, won 1925 Pulitzer Race, page 43

R3C-2
  Curtiss seaplane, piloted by Doolittle, won 1925 Schneider Cup, pages 42-43

Radar
  Americans were unsure, when planning for Doolittle raid, whether Japan had developed radar capability, pages 5, 39

Roosevelt, President Franklin D.
  Enthusiastic about Tokyo raid when presented with idea in January 1942, pages 1-2; "Shangri-la" story, pages 36-37; presented the Medal of Honor to Doolittle in June 1942, page 38

Schneider Trophy Races
  Doolittle had had some experience with Navy pilots during the Schneider Races in 1925, pages 14, 47; background to Doolittle's flying a Navy seaplane in the 1925 race, pages 42-43

Service Rivalry
  Doolittle feels Army-Navy teamwork was what caused his April 1942 Tokyo raid to succeed, pages 41-42; competition among services for resources, pages 41-42, 48-50

17th Bombardment Group
  Chosen by Doolittle to perform Tokyo raid because of their capabilities, page 11; 24 crews chosen for 16 slots in actual raid, pages 11-12

Thirty Seconds Over Tokyo
  Assessed by Doolittle as excellent movie, page 9

Williams, Lieutenant Alford J., USN
  Beaten by Army pilot in 1925 Pulitzer Race, page 43

Willows, California
  Doolittle raiders practiced takeoffs at Willows in early 1942 before joining carrier Hornet (CV-8), page 13

York, Captain Edward J., USA
  Difficulties during April 1942 Tokyo raid, page 33

www.ingramcontent.com/pod-product-compliance
Lightning Source LLC
Chambersburg PA
CBHW080609170426
43209CB00007B/1382